Black Misery

and other

Slave Songs

Poems and Short Stories of the

African Diaspora

To Suzanne,
Thank you so much.
— Toretha
9-24-22

Black Misery

and other

Slave Songs

Poems and Short Stories of the African Diaspora

Toretha Wright

Black Misery and other Slave Songs
Copyright © 2019 by Toretha Wright
All rights reserved.

No part of this book may be reproduced, stored in, or introduced into a retrieval system or transmitted in any form or by any means (electronic, mechanical photocopying, recording, or otherwise) without prior written permission from the publisher.

Publisher's Note: With the exception of the titles listed below, this is a work of fiction. Names characters places and situations either are used fictitiously or are products of the author's imagination.

True stories: *Irene's Story, Adeline Jackson's Slave Story, Joshua Corley, Sr., Queen Thompson, Great Grandma Viney and the Confederacy, and Mama Nita, A Holiness Preacher.*

Library of Congress Control Number in-publication-data
Wright Toretha 1954-

ISBN: 9781080447527

Some of the "Black Misery is…" quotes used in this publication were from aalbc.com, African American Literary Book Club. Used by permission, Troy Johnson.

Cover photo: publicdomainclip-art.blogspot.com

Published by WrightStufco, Columbia, SC
www.wrightstuf.com

Printed in the United States of America

What's Inside

Introduction
On Purpose 1
What is black misery…really? 2
Impressive! 5
Sociable Blackness...7
The Help 9
Knocking 11
Something about Elijah Craig 12
Broke..15
Bent 16
Busted 17
Broke, Bent, Busted and Leaning to the Side 18
PSA 19
Safe Love 21
What's Love Like 22
Stuck 23
slow and easy love..24
Saturday Night with My Honey 25
Sin Came 27
Easter Sunday Morning 28
Keep Me Close to You, Lord 29

What We All Need!..31

…here in these united states 33

Born That Way 37

50!..38

The Gift..40

Off Track 41

If Her Apron Could Talk 43

I Know I Came from Somewhere 45

The Knowlton Place...47

What Aunt Lillian said...54

Irene's Story 55

Adeline Jackson's Slave Story 57

Joshua Corley, Sr..63

Queen Thompson 65

Great-Grandma Viney and the Confederacy...............67

Mama Nita, a Holiness Preacher 71

About the Author..76

A Note from the Author 77

Black Misery is...

...*when you heard on the radio that the neighborhood you live in is a slum, but you always thought it was home.*

~ **Langston Hughes from his book,** *Black Misery*

Introduction

When I decided to write this book, I was torn between a strict book of prose or a litany of short poems about the existence or subsistence of black people in America. It's 2019, I felt I had to write something on our 400 years of survival ...

At the time of this book's first printing, I was still not sure, but I had to publish what was in my heart at that time. It was the right thing to do for my conscience and my ancestors. Afterall, it had been 400 years.

Because I don't know from where I came, I thought about my parents and grandparents, and my great-grandparents and great-great grandparents who were born... here in these united states.

Years ago, I conducted some research on these elusive people of whom I knew very little about. Even my parents' stories about them seemed obscure so the quest provided confirmation. My dad told me stories of his parents; sharecroppers on a farm deep in the Aiken County woods. Nonetheless they were abstract figures in my young show-and-tell world.

My great-grandma Viney, who was a pressed soldier of the Confederacy, seemed real to me, however. Because so much storytelling and research has been done on her exploits, it was as if I knew her.

Grandma Queen, my father's mother, was a comprehensible character in my life's narrative since I heard him tell stories about her. She, I hear, was a mean lady, implying, she said what she meant and meant what she said. I'd listened to other anecdotes provided by my aunts, uncles and older cousins who knew her.

Although I never met my Grandma Queen or Grandpa Josh, I was blessed to spend time with Mama Nita, my mother's mom until I turned 18. I never had to guess or imagine what she was like, her concrete self, showed me her calming joy.

Since the first printing of this book, I've gathered my thoughts, my memories, and my research. This republication gives me pleasure to present more Poems and Short Stories on the African Diaspora.

1619...

We African Americans are not descendants of slaves, but are the inheritors of enslaved Africans with a rich and vibrant history, and for many, yet to be uncovered

...2019

On Purpose

Stolen

Placed in chains

Tossed in the bottom of a ship

Fed very little food and water

Swallowed up in filth and the stench

Taken to a strange land

Sold to the highest bidder

Whipped

Labored from sun-up to sun-down

Raped

Separated from family

Quasi-freed

Feared

Mis-educated

Yet with tenacity, strength, and a will to survive

We've lasted 400 years

On Purpose

What is black misery…really?

Black misery is a wonder, an intangible
It's different for all of us,
Yet it's the same ball of tainted yarn
For those who try to inflict it …
Like being told you're 3/5 of a whole person
But you know you have the same amount of parts
As everyone else...
A heart,
a soul,
a thinking mind.

What is black misery…
The misery that some said
The reality of our ancestors' enslavement
Was a *necessary evil*
Because of finances and fear,
And when confronted with an unsuccessful secession.
Slavery was replaced with
Sharecropping,
Convict leasing,
Mass incarceration, and
Reality TV

The misery of being black is abstract
When you know your poverty
Has nothing to do with your worth.

But systemic redlining,
Gentrification,
And plain old racism
Has all to do with it.

Black Misery is…

…seeing the children of the Diaspora equating "making it" in America with expensive material possessions such as the fabulous house and car while forgetting that finding peace within their soul is the only way to "make it" anywhere on the globe.

~ G. Les Malone

Impressive!

Got a big student loan and finished college!
Outstanding!
A big company offered me a job with a big salary, too!
Impressive!
Black American Express card came in the mail today!
Outstanding!
Mortgaged a big brick house over in Magnolia Hills!
Impressive!
Signed the papers for the Audi Q7 3.0 Prestige!
Outstanding!
Took two weeks' vacation in Cancun with friends!
Marvelous!
But I have this worn-out feeling of
polarization
living in
desperation
trying to fit into a world of
complication
with no
sensation
and lonely
expectation.
But I'm impressive!

Black Misery is...

... dividing ourselves because we are 'too dark' or 'too light' skinned when our hearts pump just the same.

~ S. Neil

Sociable Blackness

Lizzy stood tall
She had to --
Who was going to stand tall for her?
Poor girl - Mama gone - Papa, too

Lizzy's thick hair smelled of Royal Crown
Her legs shined from a good helping of Crisco
Her clothes showed some wear
But they were clean and pressed

Her hands, rough like Mama's
From scrubbing and washing and ironing
Lizzy can cook too
Food fit for a king
She baked a pie
For Dr. King and Mr. Abernathy
Once
When they were over at Miss Verdell's house
Talking about marching for civil rights
Miss Verdell said he ate two pieces

Lizzy turned eighteen
They say she should've been married by now
But the town boy didn't like dark skin
Sad
His skin was dark too
Lizzy took the Greyhound bus to Brooklyn
She packed fried chicken and pound cake
For the long ride
A new big city

More to see
More to love
More to see who might love her, too

Lizzy got a job scrubbing, washing, and ironing
In Apartment 10 A
She fit in because she kept her talk to a minimum
Mama had said,
"Use your eyes and your ears more than your mouth
And listen to what's being said around you
That's how you learn and get paid."

The rich missy in Apartment 10 A
Was doing wrong things with the rich mister
Down in Apartment 10 C
Lizzy looked, listened, learned
She got paid because she kept her talk to a minimum

Lizzy got paid enough to move up to a new place,
Apartment 10 B
New friends came around
Men friends too
Lizzie's thick hair was pressed and curled
Her clothes were new
Legs shined with silk stockings
Lizzy found out the city boys like dark skin
Lizzy liked her dark skin, too.

The Help

She wore natural hair
Face bare
Full lips
Wide hips
Thick thighs
Large, dark, dreamy eyes
Never a smile
Strolling down the grocery store aisle
Holding the hand of another woman's child

Black Misery is...

...when I see our "Natural Conscious" Brothas & Sistas locked and wrapped tight, speaking about the plight of our cause. With nicotine and alcohol dangling from their hands. Talking the talk but not walking the walk.

~ RJ Haynes

Knocking

Long hair knocking short hair
Knocking locks and braids
Light skin knocking dark skin
Wasting time
Ostracizing
Criticizing
Separating
Demonizing
And sidestepping what really matters
Not understanding that someday
We will all be dead
And shut up in a grave somewhere.

Something about Elijah Craig

There was something about Elijah Craig
That had Mattie Jones looking very, very bad
Life for her had been just sad
Stumbling down a dark rocky road
Carrying that heavy load
Taking three steps back
And never getting on track
It had gotten that desperate
She just settled for less
She was in a terrible state
She was a mess

Elijah Craig was from Kentucky
At least that's what they say
He offered vain promises
That made a woman's day
But the feel-good feeling
Never lasted very long
Mattie was doing fine at first
Then something went very wrong

Mattie was weak
And Elijah Craig knew it
They all cried out
Why did you let Elijah do it?
There was nothing else left

After the years of abuse
Frazzled and worn down,
Her mind had long been gone
And of no good use

Mattie Jones lost everything;
Home, relationships, even her soul
There was a light at the end of the tunnel, though
A train coming towards her
Big and bold
It was the old departure train
With no return tickets sold
I guess that was the only way to free her
From that awful hold

Here's a warning to all
Stay away from the others
When you hear them call
They will take away your hope
They will make you fall
Jack Daniels, Evan Williams, Jim Beam
And their liar friend
Who goes by the name of Johnny Walker Red or Black
Depending on the mood you're in

Black Misery is…

……living paycheck to paycheck, going to a job that you hate, and the boss hates you, but you have bills, so you endure, all while praying for a lottery win in the name of Jesus…

~Toretha Wright, July 2019

Broke

I was broke
And wanted to buy something new
But the bills are way overdue
Rent man wants his money too.

Bent

I was already bent
But I got me something to drink
They said gin makes your nature rise
But I aint got nobody
Since the seal wasn't broke
I took it back to the liquor store

Busted

I was busted
But I went shopping last night
Charged a new dress and some high heel shoes
Problem is ...
I aint got nowhere to go

Broke, Bent, Busted and Leaning to the Side

Yesterday I was broke
Last night I was bent
I got my check, paid my rent
I'm bout busted, so I went to the liquor store
Charged me some gin
Put on my new dress and high heel shoes
I might be broke, bent, and busted
But I'm just a strutting
And leaning to the side

PSA

Do you or someone you know
Have a problem with drinking?
Learn the warning signs
And really get to thinking

You and your loved ones
Lives may one day depend
On the value you place on
That bottle of gin

Don't take life for granted
It's way too risky
To live your life
In a bottle of whiskey

Black Misery is...

...loving someone so hard, giving everything you have, emotionally and physically, and finding out he has no intentions of loving you back ...

~Toretha Wright

Safe Love

Our love was quiet and still
Undisturbed and safe
But is that love?

Love was meant to be explored
Nurtured and imagined
Anticipated and participating.

Without these attributes,
It's merely two sad souls subsisting together
With neither fault nor feeling
Passive and pathetic
Not worthy of being called love

What's Love Like

Love is like the weather
You can't control it
All you can do is sit back and wait for it to pass
And hope it doesn't do you any harm in the meantime
It can be sunny one day and a vicious tornado the next
Destroying everything alive and healthy
And making it weak and unpleasant

On sunny days love can be wonderful
You'll see love in the flowers and the trees
Smell it in the dewdrops and the air you breathe
Hear it in the bird's song
And feel it in your lover's kiss

But the sun doesn't show up every day
Without some dark clouds
And neither does Love
All you can do is hope the clouds don't stay too long
So, you can enjoy the little bit of sunshine you get

Stuck

They loved without thinking.
But who thinks
When you are in love?
Especially when the loving is sweet
Like homemade wine.

They loved hard on one another.
When you saw one
You likely saw the other.
One day they looked up
And the love was gone.

Through the babies and the bills,
And thoughts of running away in the middle of the night;
Leaving only a note and bad memories.
They decided to stick together and
Weather the storm and the bad memories.

One day they looked up
And the chaos of running their lives
Soon cleared.
With minds clear, they were freed from the mess
And love found them, again.

slow and easy love

The summer moon was full and bright
Bound by a dark and starless night
His body cast an unforgettable shadow
As he stood in the moonlight over her bed

His eyes were as bright as the moon, too
Staring down at her
She lifted the cover and moved over
Just enough to let him slide in beside her

He pulled her closer to his body
And she was hot like fire
She let out a soft moan so not to disturb the young'un
Lying next to her
He rolled over and let love takeover

She felt like silk cover
So smooth and gentle
Their love flowed slow and easy
Like a well-played blues song
Until the morning sun peeped through the window

"Get up!
Hurry now!
That cotton aint gon pick itself!"

Saturday Night with My Honey

We slaved 'til the rain came down hard
The rain took over the cotton field
We ran inside the cabin; soaked and cold
In quiet emotion, we listened to the rain hit the tin roof
With soothing and mellow drops as we rested

Pots and pans captured water from the leaks
And joined in the rain dance melody
In a little while, we mopped up the overflow
And covered the bed with old cotton sheets
Worn out from love's sweat and tears

With fresh rainwater captured
We cleaned the day's work off our bodies
Quiet, naked, alone, and still
We enjoyed the freedom that comes with
A Saturday night rain

Black misery is…

…watching Black Churches die because many members are ashamed of praising the God that brought us all through, when society thought we were doomed.

~ Lady J

Sin Came

Sin came to Sunday Lane
The blind led the blind
And no one had a cane…

Sin came to the young and the old
Confusing the head
And demeaning the soul

Some made it out while many fell
Through plea and prayer
By way of high water and hell

Sin often came to Sunday Lane
And stirred up the flesh
Again and again

Easter Sunday Morning

Sitting in church
On the very last pew
Folks turning around
Fake smiling at you

Singing's getting good
Preaching is too
You feel like shouting
But folk keep looking at you

Your leg starts shaking
You don't know what to do
But your soul takes over
And you're shouting Hallelu

While you're jumping and crying
Here comes altar call
So, you're walking down the aisle
And your cigarettes fall

You're feeling so uncomfortable
You wanna just curse
But the usher hands them to you
And you stick them in your purse

You give your life to God
While you're wiping away the tears
This time you mean it…
Same as the last few years

Keep Me Close to You, Lord

I thought I pushed my grace to the limit
Making vain promises I knew I couldn't keep
Though my mind and heart was truly willing
My human flesh was just scorned and weak

I'm kneeling and praying every day
For God to take these desires away
Yet, within, my heart is not ready to be free
This worldly lust has the best of me

Still, I ask Him to hold me and keep me
And don't let me stray too much
I pray that this desire will someday leave me
Until then, God sustain me with Your loving touch

Black Misery is...

...giving up on lifelong goals and taking menial jobs because we are scared to dream the impossible (or is it?) dream.

~ S. Neil

What We All Need!

(A Cry for Humility)

Just living not giving…
Work every day to pay for what I say I need
Indeed, God said don't worry
He has my back
But sometimes I act like His stuff is just not enough for my greed

I want to serve my fellow man…
To do what I can
But understand I'm mostly about self…
What about me?
I say when I need to be lending a hand to someone else

Excuse after excuse I give on why I'm not philanthroping
While I sit around
Facebooking
Candy crushing
Doing Nothing
But looking to be entertained on the big screen

Ungrateful for what I got…
God's grace and mercy should be enough to sustain me
But I act like it's not

I'm not alone on this selfish quest

Thinking we are the world's best
However, knowing we are all just spoiled
The young, the old, and in-betweens…
Acting like we are all kings and queens…

But I'm trying to put aside this selfish greed
Understanding that
HUMILITY IS WHAT WE ALL NEED!

...here in these united states

    Sunday morning
Woke up to blood on my television...
Widescreen...
Wide scene
People running...
Police gunning...
Down... here in these united states.

    Monday morning
Went into my office of silent majority...
Heads down
Surely, I'm not the only one with widescreen...
But another brother
Broke the ice
Looking for advice...
"What's Going On?" ... here in these united states

    Tuesday morning
Still silence...
No eye contact
Just back...
Back of the head...
Back of the mind...
Get to the back of the line... here in these united states

    Wednesday morning
I'm still dazed
Unamazed at the outward pouring of apathy
Knowing that you are
Just as sad as me... here in these united states

    Thursday mourning
Trayvon Martin, Dontre Hamilton, Eric Garner,
John Crawford III, Michael Brown, Ezell Ford,
Laquan McDonald, Akai Gurley, Tamir Rice,
Antonio Martin, Jerame Reid, Tony Robinson,
Charley Leundeu Keunang, Anthony Hill,
Meagan Hockaday, Eric Harris, Walter Scott,
Freddie Gray, William Chapman, Jonathan Sanders,
Botham Jean, Atatiana Jefferson, etc., etc., etc…

    Friday mourning
Charlottesville, Sutherland Springs Church, The
Charleston Nine, Sandra Bland, Samuel DuBose, Jeremy
McDole, Corey Jones, Jamar Clark, Bruce Kelley Jr.,
Alton Sterling, Philando Castile, Joseph Mann,
Abdirahman Abdi, Paul O'Neal, Korryn Gaines, Sylville
Smith, Terence Crutcher, Keith Lamont Scott, Alfred
Olango, Deborah Danner, Columbine, Sandy Hook,
Stoneman Douglas, Virginia Tech, El Paso, Philly,
Vegas, L.A. (Insert your city here), etc., etc., etc…

Saturday mourning
It's been a rough week here in these united states
People are dying
Mothers and others are crying
I'm sitting here sighing
About the latest slaying
Need to be praying
Before it's too late
Understanding that there is too much hate
Here in these united states.

Black Misery is…

…*living.*

~ Toretha Wright

Born That Way

Lord, Little Richard Walker was so gay
I truly believe he was born that way
I mean those switching hips when he walked
And the wispy lisp when he talked

I think he was like that from the very start
His feminine ways were engraved in his heart
So I'm not far off the mark when I say what I say
Little Richard Walker was born that way

Many disagree with what I have said
They think it's a choice, and all in his head
A demon, they tell me, can be rooted out
With the help of the Good Lord, no doubt

But, the truth is the truth and I still say
This little boy was surely born that way
No two ways about it, and fact is fact
To be born gay or straight is a natural act

We're all God's children, no matter how we're born
No one should be subjected to ridicule or scorn
And even if I'm wrong, I still don't lose
God says love everyone, we don't get to choose

50!

Mrs. Roberts humbly reached the half-century mark.
An achievement in itself.
Aside from the AARP subscription letters
That flooded her mailbox,
She felt no difference from 49.
She was the same energetic careerist and volunteer
With more things to get done than the hours in a day.

The younger women gave her apologetic looks.
You know the look of condolence.
As if she would live only a few more weeks.
She smiled and thought, *You should be so lucky.*
Others proudly announced,
"You sure don't look fifty."
She gasped,
Unable to grasp how 50 was supposed to look.

She knew other half-centenarians
But how does one characterize how a woman
In her 50s
Should look, act, or feel?

Were there schematic groupings somewhere
That segmented each decade until age 60?
And then, are we placed into a whole new category
Of how we should
Look, feel, and act at …
60, 70, 80…?

What annoyed her more?
Her peers,
Her half-century tribe.
"You know 50 is the new 30," they told her.
"Nonsense," she replied.

"At 30,
I could see better,
I didn't need reading glasses,
Or bifocals or the little magnifier
I carry in my purse.

At 30, I didn't groan,
While getting up from a sofa or chair,
Or just plain getting up in the morning.
At 30, my waist was smaller,
Hips slimmer,
Chin, arms, and thighs firmer,
And I wasn't looking forward to retiring…
As much.
There were no hot flashes and night sweats, like
"Fire shut up in my bones."

"No," she continued,
50 is not 30;
Physically, emotionally, or practically"

So, when she hears that tired old phrase,
"Fifty is the New Thirty,"
She just smiles because she realizes its vain attempt
To feel a little bit better about the inevitable…
That we will get old someday…if we're lucky.

The Gift

I remember apple trees, the biting cold air, and the old lady who lived downstairs. The snowsuit; the color of which has faded in my memory, but it could have been red.

Looking down at the others through the spindles in the railing on the second-floor landing of the boarding house, I remember I was troubled back then.

Who doo child, Mama'd called me. But she also called me blessed. She knew. Because a mother knows her child. Even when she can't change what God "gifts" to her children, she tries to protect them the best she knows how.

I was three. I had a broad understanding of life even then. Mama said it was because of the veil I had on my face at birth. She knew. The midwife knew too.

I could sense things in people. Things that were not good. That was a heavy enough burden for an adult to carry; let alone a child. I'd lose it if I could.

I knew that bad people with evil spirits lived all around us. Taking in our air and breathing out wicked air so the weak could succumb to the evilness of the world.

I was afraid to know these things back then, so I suppressed the gift ...until now.

Off Track

When I was about eight, my older sister told me that the earth was moving closer to the sun, and one day it would explode into a billion pieces of stardust.

"No way," I said. "But just in case, I'll move to the North Pole and live with Santa. But I thought, I really didn't want to live with that fat white man and a bunch of pointy-eared, weird-looking little people. Plus, he seemed to love those reindeer just a bit too much. And where in the world was Mrs. Claus? You rarely saw her; only in those photos ops.

My sister said, "You're stupid. The North Pole is part of the earth anyway. It'll be caught up in the explosion."

I rethought that North Pole move, and said, "I'll take my chances with the sun.

Years later, I heard Joni Mitchell's song "Woodstock" ...

We are stardust. Billion-year-old carbon. We are golden. Caught in the devil's bargain. And we've got to get ourselves back to the garden.

With all the misery in this world, it would be nice to get back to the garden.

Black Misery is...

...*not recognizing our ancestors for the heroes they were. Slaves who fought and taught us how to endure through their will. The ones who didn't give up, but maintained... for future generations to come forth and be proud men and women who will refuse to belong to anyone or anything."*

~ Toretha Wright

If Her Apron Could Talk

(A Confederate Slave Soldier)

I thought about her the other day
She must have been a very good cook for him to take her
The pain she must have felt in the deep cold at night
Or the southern heat of the day
No shelter
Just tin pans and oil and her apron

That old apron must have been dingy too
From wiping flour and cooking oil, hands and brow sweat
I thought about the sticky briar patches she walked through
Being careful of poison oak and ivy

If Her Apron Could Talk
Would it tell us her mood when she picked dandelion greens and mushrooms when the rations got low?
Would it tell us how she longed to go home?
Be with the familiar no matter how oppressed

If Her Apron Could Talk
Would it say what went on out there? Was she warm?
What came to my mind was the picture of Harriett Tubman hanging on my wall

With her long skirt and warm coat
She was poised and self-confident
Shotgun in one hand and a big stick in the other
Ready to fight if she had too

I thought about her in that apron
With no poise or self-confidence
No stick or shotgun
Unsafe from animals - and humans
Was she protected?
Someone had to have protected her
Of course, she had no firearm just tin pans and oil
Yes, God protected her

Oh, if her apron could talk
Would it tell of the honor in doing what she was called to do?
Yes, I think if that old apron could talk it would say,

"I've seen hard times
But I've seen some good ones too
I've been rebuked and
I've been scorned
But I've been loved too
I've handled my business
I've been used for my purpose.
Now it's time to lay me down
So, I can rest!"

I Know I Came from Somewhere

(The Slave Child's Song)

I know I came from somewhere
But the whereabouts unknown
It was a far-off land I know
I feel it deep down in here
I know I'm someone special
My mama made that clear
But the master he don't know it
See these scars I wear
He takes me in his room at night
And knows me while I sleep
He makes me warm his belly
But I'm much too short to reach
Mama cries *Don't you worry child*
That sin is for him to hold
He can touch you all the long while
But he will never have your soul
Mama hugs me when I'm crying
Saying *Girl don't shed no tear*
I been fixing him some special tea

And soon he'll be gone from here

Last night when he called for me

To come to his master bed

Mama didn't wait for tea no more

She stabbed him now he's dead

Now Mama and me are on the run

And the dogs are close at hand

I wonder if we'll ever be free

To see that far-off land

I've lived twelve blue moons so far

Don't know how many more I'll see

I know I came from somewhere

That somewhere lives in me

The Knowlton Place

Elnora Mathis relaxed on the grand veranda that stood on the front grounds of the Knowlton Home. Funny, she still called it that seeing that she had just bought the home and its furnishings and the 10 acres that surrounded it at an estate sale.

No one had lived in the old house for years. And some town folks didn't like an outsider coming in outbidding them for that prime piece of property either. And an *old colored woman* at that. But Elnora wasn't an outsider and she surely didn't think that she was old. As a matter of fact, she had grown up in Hamilton County. Right there on the Knowlton Place where she was born - inside the small cottage that still stood far behind the main house. She had lived there with her mama, papa, and grandma and all of her twelve siblings who had a hand in maintaining that great big estate she now called home. Newly retired from the 'big city' that wasn't always kind to a woman living alone, she found it necessary to move back home to her roots. Now, that prime piece of property was all hers.

Early morning, when the birds were awake singing their hearts out, was the best time for her to sit out on the veranda. The cool breeze and the dampness from the morning dew stirred up memories from when she was just a girl. The big white gabled house with the wrap-around porch; the large beds of colorful begonias, petunias, marigolds, and other colorful flowers that blanketed both sides of the house were in rare form that summer. Showy, like they were modeling in a fashion show for those who passed down the long country road. She remembered that some of the flowers needed to be watered at sundown and others at sun-up. The rows of large magnolia trees that bared fruit and large flowers every year all belonged to Elnora, too. The Magnolias were an integral part of her Southern landscape. Sometimes they bloomed in early spring before the leaves developed, but this year they waited to flower in summer when the foliage was full. Either way, Elnora sat peacefully outside, enjoying it all and remembering what her Mama told her, "White magnolia flowers stand for purity and perfection, just like us Mathis women."

She glanced over the expanse of her land, as far as her eyes could take her. Apple, peach, pear and other fruit trees stood tall among the pecan and hickory nut trees that also laced the property throughout. Though dense virgin forest (rebirthed from the last hurricane) surrounded the outer perimeters, she felt safe from the outside world. Blessed that she could commune with God from the veranda of the big house instead of the cottage she'd known so well in her youth.

The Mathis women had nurtured that big old house for more than one hundred and fifty years, starting with her great-grandmother, a fourteen-year-old slave girl who withstood more than her share of misery. The property was passed down through the generations and so did the people who worked there over the years. Alongside her Mama and sisters, Elnora treated the house as if it had belonged to them. Caring for the hardwood floors, making them shine like a brand-new automobile. Using just a pinch of white vinegar in her cleaning water, Elnora made the crystal chandelier that hung in the dining room glitter like diamonds and the old porcelain tubs sparkled like new. How amazing, she thought. All that labor and devotion paid off.

Elnora heard a caravan of automobiles driving up the dirt road that led to her home. As they got closer, she heard the busy chatter and laughter of men, women, and children. She remembered the church volunteers who had insisted they help with the renovations. Elnora was puzzled when they had come by earlier in the week while she sat in the same comfortable chair on the veranda. They noticed that she was alone. "You married?" the man asked.

"No, widowed."

"Chirren?"

"They're grown and on their own. Why you ask?"

"I know some people who can make this place look like new with a few coats of paint and a few wood boards," the man said.

Elnora had agreed, reluctantly. Not wanting to seem ungrateful for the gesture of church folk doing Good Samaritan work for the Lord. Who was she to say 'no' to God's people? On second thought, maybe they were just nosey.

"Good morning." Elnora greeted the visitors with her usual cheerful voice, although she was a bit perturbed. She wanted to enjoy the peace and quiet of a warm country morning.

"Good morning, Miss Elnora. It's a nice morning. Isn't it? Not a cloud in the sky."

"Yes, it's a very nice morning."

"I'm Pastor Dan, and these are some of our young people. Our volunteer summer workers from the Methodist Church down the road apiece."

"Nice to meet you." Elnora adjusted the brim on her wide straw hat to get a good look at the man.

"We're here to get started on fixing up the place." He extended his hand and lightly gripped hers.

Twelve or so young people mumbled lazy good mornings. Three women from a big older modeled car, not dressed for work, pulled out coolers and food baskets. One whispered, "It's a shame she bought this big old house and all alone."

"Maybe Social Services can send someone over to help her out," said another one.

Shaking their heads, the women set the baskets and the coolers on the steps.

Pastor Dan and the youth unloaded buckets of paint, lumber, ladders, and small utility bags from one of the trucks. "You just continue enjoying your morning, Miss Elnora," he said.

The white paint that once dressed the large house in grand style had all but peeled away. Some of the floorboards on the porch had rotted away in some places and would soon be fitted with new ones. The porch railings were rickety, but nothing a few nails and screws couldn't fix. Noisily, they painted, puttied, screwed, and spackled, filling in cracks and crevices; a generous effort to restoring the exterior of the house to its fine grandeur.

Elnora, realizing that they had worked for nearly four hours, insisted that they break for lunch and return the next day. It was summer, and the kids needed to enjoy it. The group packed up the trucks, and the youth were glad they had the afternoon free. Pastor Dan and the women were curious about the interior of the house, however. He wondered how much work they needed to do inside. As the group entered the home, they gazed at the splendor of it all; in complete surprise that the hardwood floors shine like new. The crystal chandeliers sparkled like the stars at night. The wallpaper, although obviously old, showed no signs of age or wear - just crisp and the furniture was pristine. One woman asked snobbishly, "How can this be? Elnora is as blind as a bat. There is no way she could have gotten this raggedy old house into this good of shape this quick. It's only been 10 days. Plus she's old."

Another one said, "Yes. I've been watching the place, and no repairmen or cleaning service or visitors have been here at all."

Pastor Dan replied, "Now ladies, be kind. Miss Elnora is not completely blind. But you're right. This house is too clean. It's like folks been living here all along."

They looked around; checking for dust and dirt. As they strolled on towards the kitchen, a light came on, and a loud voice resounded from what seemed like out of nowhere, *"WE MATHIS WOMEN HAVE BEEN TAKING CARE OF THIS HOUSE FOR OVER 150 YEARS!"*

The inquisitive church workers quickly turned around and ran out the front door. Without as much as a "See you later," they jumped in their automobiles and sped back down the dirt road away from the Knowlton Place, leaving a cloud of dust behind them. Elnora watched the group heave so hurriedly without saying goodbye. A woman, clad in a starched white apron, emerged from the kitchen, making her way to the front door. "Elnora," she called out. "Where did your company go?"

"I don't know, Sister," Elnora said with a broad smile on her face. "They just left like they saw a ghost."

"Crazy church folks," Sister said laughing, as she got ready to head back to her little cottage at the back of the house where she had lived for going on sixty-nine years. "Elnora, come on in now; lunch is ready."

Elnora pushed her way up from the soft-cushioned chair and with her cane in one hand and a microphone in the other, she said, "HOLD YOUR HORSES, I'M COMING."

Yes, the Mathis women have always lived on the Knowlton Place and would continue to live there and take care of it for years to come.

What Aunt Lillian said

I'm 96 years old and some
I've lived a long full life
I believe I did what was good and right
As a mother and a dear wife

I left my mark on this old world
In some way, form or fashion
I believe I did some good things
I know I showed compassion

I made a difference to someone
As I traveled life's rough road
I know I carried a lot of burdens
Including my own heavy load

I did some sinful work too, I know
I'm not proud of that fact
But God didn't make us all
To live so perfectly intact

And when He comes to take me home
I'll know I've been well blessed
So I'll shut my weary old eyes
And let God sort out the rest.

Irene's Story

Excerpt from Slave Narratives - Interview with Irene Coates

The overseer on the plantation was very hard on the slaves and practiced striking them across the back with a whip when he wanted to spur them on to do more work. One day, a crowd of women were hoeing in the field and the overseer rode along and struck one of the women across the back with the whip. The one nearest her spoke and said that if he ever struck her like that, it would be the day he or she would die. The overseer heard the remark and the first opportunity he got, he rode by the woman and struck her with the whip and started to ride on. The woman was hoeing at the time; she whirled around, struck the overseer on his head with the hoe, knocking him from his horse, and she then pounced upon him and chopped his head off. She went mad for seconds and proceeded to chop and mutilate his body; that done to her satisfaction. She then killed his horse. She then calmly went to tell the master of the murder, saying, "I've done killed de overseer."

The master replied, "Do you mean to say you've killed the overseer?"

She answered yes, and that she had killed the horse also.

Without hesitating, the master pointing to one of his small cabins on the plantation said, "You see that house over there?"

She answered yes at the same time looking.

"Well," said he, "take all your belongings and move into that house and you are free from this day and if the mistress wants you to do anything for her, do it if you want to."[i]

Adeline Jackson's Slave Story

Excerpt from Slave Narratives *Interview with Adeline Jackson, 88 years old*

"I was born four miles southwest of where I is now, on the other side of Woodward Station. I was a slave of old Master John Mobley, the richest man, the larges' landowner, and with more niggers than any other white man in the county. He was the seventh son of the seventh son, so he allowed, and you knows that's a sign of a big family, lots of cows, mules, horses, money, chillun and everything that's worth having'.

He had a good wife too; dis the way he got her, he say. She the daughter of old Maj. Andy McLean, who got a body full of bullets in the Revolution; he didn't want Katie to marry Master John. Master John git on a mule and ride up in the night. Miss Katie runned out, jump up behind' him, run away and marry Master John. They had the same birthday, March 27th, but Master John two years older than Miss Katie. That day was looked to, same as Christmas, every year that come. Big times then, I tell you!

"My mistress had long hair, techin' the floor and could dance, so Master John said, with a glass of water on top of her head. Master John got religion and went all the way like the jailer in the Bible. All the house joined with him and most of the slaves. It was Baptist and he built a spankin' good church building' down the road, all out of his own money, and the cemetery there yet. He called it 'Fellowship.' Some fine tombstones in there yet. The finest cost two thousand dollars, that's his daughter Nancy's tomb. Master John and my old mistress buried in there.

"When my youngest' mistress, name Marion Rebecca, married her second cousin, Master Edward P. Mobley, I was give to her and went with them to the June place. It was called that because old Doctor June built it and sold it to Master Ed. I nursed her first chillun: Edward, Moses Hill, John and Katie. It was a large, two-story frame house, with chimneys at each gable end. Master Edward got to be as rich as old master; he owned the June place, the Rochelle plantation, the Peay place and the Roebuck place. Yes sir, course us had overseers for so many slaves and plantations. I 'member Mr. Oze Brown, Mr. Neely and Mr. Tim Gladney. In course of time I was took off the nursing' and put to the field. I dropped cotton seed, hoed some, and picked cotton.

"I don't remember no poor buckra, outside the overseers, except a Mr. Reed that lived down on Wateroe, passing our house sometime. He was a Godforsaken looking man that master or mistress always give something.

"Our neighbors was the Pearys, the Durhams, the Picketts, the Barbers and Boulwares. Doctor Henry Gibson was our doctor. All these folks kept' a pack of hounds to run deer and foxes. Yes, I has eat many pieces of deer. Good? I wouldn't fool you, taste it and you'll hunger for it ever afterward.

"Yes sir, at certain times we worked long and hard, and you had to be particular. The only whipping I got was for chopping down a good corn stalk near a stump in a new ground. Master never sold a slave, but swaps were made with kin people to advantage, slaves' wives and husbands sometimes.

I never learned to read or write. I went to White Poplar Springs Church, the Baptist church my mistress 'tended. The preacher was Mr. Cartledge. He allowed Miss Marion was the flower of his flock.

"Slaves lived in quarters, a stretch of small houses off from the White House. Patrollers often come to search for stray slaves; wouldn't take your word for it. They would search the house. If they ketch one without a pass, they whipped him. We got most our outside news Sunday at church.

When farm work was not pressing, we got all of Saturday to clean up 'round the houses, and wash and iron our clothes.

"Everything lively at Christmas time, dances with fiddles, patting' and stick rattling', but when I joined the church, I quit dancing'.

"After the war, a man came along on a red horse; he was dressed in a blue uniform and told us we was free. The Yankees that I 'members was not gentlefolks. They stole everything they could take and the meanest thing I ever see was shoats they half killed, cut off the hams, and left the other parts quivering' on the ground.

"I married Mose Jackson, after freedom, and had a boy, Henry. Last I heard, he was at Shelby, North Carolina. We had a daughter, Mary, she married Eph Brown. She had ten chillun, many gran' chillun, they's my great-gran' chillun. My mistress was a good Christian woman, she give me a big supper when I was married. Her house, during' the war, always had some sick or wounded soldier. I 'member her brother, Zed, come home with a leg gone. Her cousin, Theodore, was there with a part of his jaw gone.

My mistress could play the piano and sing the old songs. I 'members Master Theodore had trouble with the words. There was a song called 'Jaunita', 'bout a fountain. Master Theodore would try hard, but would say, every time, 'Jawneeta', and the folks would laugh but mistress never would crack a smile but just go on with another song. I thinks everybody should join the church and then live right. Have prayers in the family before' getting in the bed. It would have good change, 'specially in the towns I thinks.

"Yes, women in family way worked up to near the time, but guess Doctor Gibson knowed his business. Just before' the time, they was took out and put in the carding' and spinning' rooms.

"Yes, I see folks put irons in the fire and some throw a big chunk of fire into the yard to make the screech owl stop his scary sounds.

"Before' I forgits, Master Edward bought a slave in Tennessee just 'cause he could play the fiddle. Named him 'Tennessee Ike' and he played 'long with Ben Murray, another fiddler. Sometime all of us would be called up into the front yard to play and dance and sing for Miss Marion, the chillun and visitors. I was much happier them days than now. Maybe it won't be so bad when I gits my old age pension."[ii]

Black Misery is...

...waking up every day to continue the struggle from the day before wondering, worrying and thinking endless thoughts of not being able to take no more. Of the pain, punishment, suffering and being treated like you started a world war. But hell, all we did was take the front line, lost many of our kind in such a short period of time and to this day we don't know what they really died for.

~ Dellarekus

Joshua Corley, Sr.

Born 1880
Died 1950

Dad's Dad, the Sharecropper

Born on Thanksgiving Day, 1880, about 15 years after the signing of the Emancipation Proclamation by President Abraham Lincoln, Joshua Corley just did escape the misfortune of slavery. Still, the fourth child born to ex-slaves, Mack and Laura, my great-grand parents, would be a sharecropper working the fertile soil in the South Carolina County of Aiken. There would be no school for poor children like Josh. They would be relegated to the fields - planting or harvesting throughout the year.

Josh was a quiet and caring young man who worked long hours in the cotton fields to help feed his family. It was said that he would work so long in the cotton fields that at the end of the day his finger would be blood red from picking the cotton from the piercing bolls. But no one in the fields could fill up a sack of cotton as fast as he could.

He was a young man in his twenties before he met and married the woman with whom he would spend the rest of his life. Queen Thompson was born on

Christmas Eve in 1886, the fourth child born to Logan Thompson (b. 1834) and Elviney Corley Thompson (b. 1847) both former slaves. A strong-willed, but happy young woman from the same part of the county captured Josh's heart and that was that. It is unclear how they first met, but we can be certain that once they got together, it was forever. That union produced twelve children

Although they lived during the Depression Era, if you had asked any one of them how the depression affected them, they would ask, "What Depression?" And that was the attitude of the family. They had very little material wealth, but they were rich with love and kindness.

During their years of farming, the family sharecropped for white farm owners, Benny Cumbee, "a good white lady" by the name of Anna Hutto, Theodore Weeks in Montmorenci, Ben Williams of Hitchcock Farms also known as Cedar Grove, and Harold Cullum.

Josh was a deacon at Cedar Grove Baptist Church, Aiken, while Queen retained her membership at Smyrna Baptist, the Thompson family church. During their farming on the Hitchcock Farm, the family attended Mt. Anna Baptist Church. Josh, Queen and many of their children are buried in the Smyrna Baptist Church Cemetery, Springfield, South Carolina.

Queen Thompson

Born 1886
Died 1952

Don't Mess with Me

Grandma Queen sharecropped alongside Grandpa Josh and the twelve children. Her parents, however maintained their livelihoods otherwise; Great-grandpa Reverend Logan Thompson, a Baptist minister, carpenter and farmer and wife, Viney, a housekeeper and cook.

Grandma Queen, no doubt, learned culinary skills from her mama, and she baked the best biscuits ever. According to first cousins, Tweet and Henry, she served them warm with sweet sorghum syrup. Rumor had it she made sure her family would get food to eat whether the year produced a good crop of peas and corn or not. It was her contention that they worked hard all season, it was up to the good Lord to provide the bounty. If He saw fit to send a small crop that was no reason for her family to suffer.

My dad told me the story about Grandma Queen's love of family and tenacious mindset. During one season when the harvested crops produced less than expected, the wealthy landowner (the man who owned the farm the family sharecropped) came to the farm in his big farm truck to get his "fair" share of crops. Because of the thinness of the yields that year, the white man wanted more than what was agreed upon between him and my grandma. According to my dad, Grandma Queen came to the door, stuck her head out and said in no uncertain terms, that her children had to eat and she aint giving him no more than what he got. Dad said she gave the man such a severe "blessing out" that he left with his tail between his legs and never made such a foolish request again.

Great-Grandma Viney and the Confederacy

Born: 1844
Died: 1928

At the age of 18, Lavinia (Viney) Corley Thompson was drafted in the Confederate Army (as a cook). I know in my heart, if she had a choice, she would have forgone this proposal to join the same people who were fighting to keep her in bondage.

On October 14, 2018, I attended and took part in a memorial service for Granma Viney, instigated by the Lt. Gen. Wade Hampton Camp No 273 Sons of Confederate Veterans and the South Carolina Daughters of the Confederacy. I'd written a poem for her and I read it that same day. "If My Apron Could Talk," released some my thoughts of her. Even though I never knew her, I somehow feel her presence as a source of my strength and tenacity.

My great-granny received a military memorial service that day at Smyrna Baptist Church, complete with a confederate grave marker and a twenty-one gun salute. I wondered, if somewhere from that great beyond, she witnessed this trite "commemoration," and how she must have felt knowing these people were celebrating their vain attempt to keep her in visceral servitude. I had come to grips with being a part of this service, if nothing more than ensuring that the ceremony would be handled with dignity and respect. I still have the military flag they presented to her that day. I know Grandma Queen and my other ancestors are up in heaven together just laughing, and wondering if I'm going to burn the darn thing.

Excerpts from *African American Confederate Pensioners 1923-1925*

History's heroes are many, but often little remembered. In 1860 South Carolina's population included 291,300 white, 402,206 slave, and 9,914 free African Americans. The majority of the South Carolina work force was African American. Signing the Ordinance of Secession and firing the shot on Fort Sumter drove South Carolina to war. By 1862, visions of a short conflict, of peaceful coexistence with the Union, and of formal European intervention on behalf of the Confederate States had dimmed. South Carolina and the other Confederate States faced a lengthy struggle for survival. South Carolina needed labor-to support combat troops, to construct and maintain fortifications, to man essential industries, and to produce the foodstuffs to supply military and domestic needs.

By March 1862, Gen. R. S. Ripley was impressing low-country African Americans to complete fortifications around Charleston. Slaves between the ages of sixteen and fifty were eligible for impressments, but only one-fourth of an individual's work force could be taken at one time. The scope of the task and fear of imminent Federal advance created a steadily increasing demand for labor. On 27 April 1862, Ripley wrote Gov. Pickens, "If you want me to go on with the works in the harbor as the necessity of the time requires, you must send labor as fast as you can. I want a thousand negroes."

On 26 June, the Executive Council asked Gov. Pickens to issue a proclamation asking owners who had not contributed to send a fourth of the slaves "liable to road duty." In August, the Council extended the call for African American labor from the countryside to include incorporated municipalities." The Council and Gen. Pemberton, **Confederate** General commanding in South Carolina, disagreed about the scope of labor impressment. Pemberton wanted it statewide, while the Council preferred to limit it to the affected areas. By July, Pemberton had prevailed. At least 1800 men were requisitioned at a time; and service was usually for a month. On 18 December 1862, the South Carolina legislature passed Act #4614, creating a state agent to oversee African American labor raised under the act. In general, **Confederate** forces employed African Americans in limited capacities. Many served as **cooks** or servants.

In military camps, African Americans served as teamsters, cooks, and general servants. **The Pension Records of The South Carolina Confederate** pension applications abstracted here were tendered under the act of 1923. Although South Carolina provided a short lived disability compensation in 1866 and pension relief for regular **Confederate** soldiers as early as 1887, the state *did not recognize the service of South Carolina's African Americans until 1923. African Americans who served the Confederacy as "servants, cooks or attendants" were eligible for a pension. Additional qualifications included at least six months of service and the recommendation of the County Pension Board. These pensions could not exceed $25 annually. Many African Americans applied under the 1923 act. In 1924, however, the act was amended to include only South Carolina residents who served the state at least six months as servants or cooks. This provision eliminated laborers, teamsters, and those who served from other States and laborers impressed for work on the fortifications.* **One woman, Lavinia Thompson of Aiken, drew a pension for her service as a cook.** [iii]

Mama Nita, a Holiness Preacher

Born 1905
Died 1972

Mama Nita, the only grandparent I knew, was a True Christian Lady who never as much as mumbled a curse word. Everyone else who knew her said these same things about her, too. Her nature exuded the nine fruits of the Spirit - love, joy, peace, patience, kindness, goodness, faithfulness, gentleness and self-control.

She preached at Lockett Chapel up on Toole's Hill and lived at 559 Laurens Street, a house she inherited from one of her husbands; the same house I was born in. Mrs. Price, the mid-wife, told my mother that I was the ugliest child she'd ever seen until they took the veil from my face. The official name is a birth cowl. The Latin name is Caput galeatum, meaning "head helmet". It was really a piece of the amniotic sac still attached to my face. Some people consider it a sign of good luck. I can't speak for everyone else, but I've been blessed.

As a child, I recall Mama Nita's big back yard. Hardwood trees scattered about, a few bushes here and there and a small vegetable garden intentionally laid out in the back by the fence. We played hopscotch with squares and numbers drawn with a stick into the sandy yard while she washed clothes in a big black wash pot that sat atop a smoldering fire. She made lye soap in that same pot. Freshly washed clothes hung on a wire line that stretched lengthwise across the back yard, while a light airy breeze breathed fresh air through them.

My grandma always had a switch close by. She broke a few thin branches from one of the many flowering trees that laced the yard's perimeter. If my sister and I got out of hand, she threatened to whip us until we were sorry. She'd threaten her big brown mix-breed dog name Sandy, too. I don't remember her ever whipping any of us though.

Inside the house, the three bedrooms, a living room, and a dimly lit kitchen were cluttered with all kinds of stuff and filled with love. Uncle Hick's ham boning and Aunt Tricia's dolls and porcelain tea set allowed for tea parties on the front porch. Sometimes we'd play with paper dolls until Mama came to pick us up.

The kitchen was my favorite place in the house. Warm and cozy, the big ashy wood-fired cook stove always had some corn bread or hoecakes sitting on top or freshly baked sweet potatoes in the oven. The best part of eating the sweet potatoes was the fact that we had dug them up from Mama Nita's vacant lot a few blocks away. She fried hard-skin fatback, too.

As I grew into puberty and no longer needed the personal care of a sitter, the time I spent with Mama Nita grew less and less; relegated to the Thanksgiving and Christmas holidays when they came to dinner at our house.

After my high school graduation, I took a year off. I didn't know what I wanted to do so, I traveled a bit, worked a bit, partied some. Eventually, boredom caught up with me and I started college the following fall semester. In the meantime, Mama Nita was getting older. Mama brought her home to stay with us at night, using the excuse that it was too cold to be in that big old drafty house at night.

During this time, I really got to know my grandmother. Our conversations were intimate and far-reaching. We watched daytime soap operas. *The Young and the Restless* and *Another World* were our favorites. We grew closer as she shared stories of her young life with me. Born right around the turn of the 20th century, she was blessed (or cursed) with three marriages. I found out that although Mama Nita had been married three times, she was widowed after seven years with each spouse. She talked about her three husbands, how they were not always kind to her, but that she was a good wife in spite of it.

My grandma's words are still with me today and I heed them to the best of my "enlightened" ability. We also talked a about the bible and being born again. I took note of that talk as well. She went into the hospital in March of '72 for a surgical procedure. She never woke up from the anesthesia. I was eighteen and lost my last grandparent.

Mama Nita married her first husband, James Eugene Breland, my grandfather around the age of 18 or 19. He was just a year older. They had four children; two boys and two girls. I heard he was a handsome womanizer. From the pictures I saw of him, he was rather good-looking. She was a pretty woman, too. My fondest memories - her softness and beauty – physical and otherwise. My grandfather died when he was around 27 years old; complication of job-related pneumonia leaving her with four young children. His death certificate listed him as a press man. I googled it: *A pressman is a colloquial term for a printing machine operator. When you work as a pressman, your primary job duties include operating and maintaining printing presses.*

Mama Nita's parents, my great-grandparents, were Elliott Tyler, a painter by trade (born 1878, died April 8, 1926 of pulmonary tuberculosis) and Dora Tyler (born April 1, 1876, died on June 12, 1935 of apoplexy or cerebral hemorrhaging (a stroke). They had four daughters and one son. Dora had about twelve siblings.

Dora Tyler's parents, my great great-grandparents, were ex-slaves. Daniel Whitaker, born in 1821 and Minty Whitaker, born in Mississippi in 1844. I heard the story that Daniel was sold to a slaveowner in North Carolina. After emancipation, Minty traveled to the Carolinas in search of him. Now I'm not sure if Daniel was the man she was looking for, but he is the man that she found. Together they has about thirteen children. In the 1880 census, Daniel was listed as a day laborer from North Carolina; Minty a housekeeper from Mississippi.

About the Author

Toretha Wright lives in South Carolina with her family. Her literary works are set in small towns where her characters capture the charm of the South. This author of poetry, prose, and plays has presented her works in a myriad of venues; winning awards, and captivating audiences with her own style of literary license.

Books by the author:
Ties That Bind Us: Ivy's Passion
Souls on Fire
Reflections in a Faded Mirror
The Secrets of the Harvest
Dates and Nuts, Volume I
Shadow People
Dates and Nuts, Volume II
Black Misery and other Slave Songs

Buy these books online at www.amazon.com and other online bookstores. Look for releases of her new works in traditional and eBook formats coming soon.

Please email to torethawright@gmail.com for more information.

A Note from the Author

I have many stories in my head from chats with family members and friends, as well as strangers, who just needed a listening ear. People of varying backgrounds have shared with me their tales of love, happiness, and misery. From time to time, people will come into my life (I'm sure not by accident) and tell me fascinating accounts of their life experiences that have made me blush, smile, and even cry. Some of these stories have been carefully written on the pages of my books, but all of them are forever etched on my heart. I hope you enjoyed the poetry and short stories in my book, *Black Misery & other Slave Songs*. If you have, please drop a line or two to torethawright@gmail.com.

Peace and blessings!
Toretha Wright

i The Federal Writers' Project American Guide, (Negro Writers' Unit) Jacksonville, Florida. Viola b. Muse field worker excerpted from Slave Interview December 16, 1936 with Irene Coates.

ii **Slave Narratives,** Interview with Adeline Jackson, 88 years old* _W.W. Dixon, Winnsboro, S.C.

iii Elviny (Louvenia Corley) Thompson in the Confederate Army, Excerpts from *African American Confederate Pensioners 1923-1925* © 1998 South Carolina Department of Archives and History Editor and designer: Judith M. Andrews Acknowledgements -- Many thanks to Lee Drago of our Publications Advisory Board, who suggested this publication. The author gratefully acknowledges the assistance of Dolly 'Wells, Ruth Green, Marion Chandler, Garry Davis, Judith Andrews, and Tim Belshaw. Also, Patrick McCawley shared his Civil War records expertise, and Joseph Gainey contributed material on upstate pensioners.

Made in the USA
Columbia, SC
18 February 2020